GRASSLANDS

Mary-Jane Wilkins

BROWN BEAR BOOKS

Published by Brown Bear Books Ltd

4877 N. Circulo Bujia
Tucson, AZ 85718
USA

and

First Floor
9–17 St Albans Place
London N1 0NX

ISBN 978-1-78121-362-9

Library of Congress Cataloging-in-Publication
Data available on request

Picture Researcher: Clare Newman
Designer: Melissa Roskell
Design Manager: Keith Davis
Editorial Director: Lindsey Lowe
Children's Publisher: Anne O'Daly

Printed in China

Picture Credits

The photographs in this book are used by
permission and through the courtesy of:

Front Cover: tl, ©Shutterstock/Zikovec; cl,
©Shutterstock/Ehrman Photographic; br,
©Shutterstock/Nick Fox; c, ©Shutterstock/
Volodymyr Burdiak; br, ©Shutterstock/Eris
Isselee.
Inside: 1, ©Shutterstock/Zlikovee; 4,
©Shutterstock/Svetlana Foote; 4-5, ©Shutterstock
/Lorimer Images; 6, ©Shutterstock/Magay
Mayer; 6-7, ©Shutterstock/Jez Bennett; 8,
©Shutterstock/2630ben; 8-9, ©Shutterstock/
Nickolay Stanev; 10, ©Shutterstock/Donovan
Van Staden; 10-11, ©Shutterstock/David Steele;
12, ©Shutterstock/Palenque; 13, ©Shutterstock/
Mauricio S. Ferreira; 14, ©Shutterstock/
Geraldb; 14-15, ©Shutterstock/Stuart G. Porter;
16, ©Shutterstock/Curioso; 17, ©Shutterstock/
Image Focus; 18, ©Nature PL/Anup Shah; 18-19,
©Shutterstock/Ioflo69; 20, ©Shutterstock/Nick
Fox; 21, ©Shutterstock/Ellie 1; 22, ©Shutterstock/
Long Tail Dog; 23, ©Shutterstock/Sergey
Uryadnikov.
T=Top, C=Center, B=Bottom, L=Left, R=Right

Brown Bear Books has made every attempt to
contact the copyright holder. If you have any
information please contact:
licensing@brownbearbooks.co.uk

CONTENTS

Where Are the Grasslands? 4

Lion 6

Zebra 8

Elephant 10

Vulture 12

Burrowing Owl 13

Cheetah 14

Wildebeest 16

Hyena 18

Przewalski's Horse 19

Prairie Dog 20

Grasslands Facts 22

Useful Words 23

Find Out More 24

Index 24

Where Are the GRASSLANDS?

Grasslands grow in many places around the world. Tropical grasslands grow in places that are hot all year round. Temperate grasslands grow in places that are cold in winter.

Grasslands in North America are called prairies. This bald eagle lives there.

In the tropical grasslands in Africa grasses grow 7 feet (2 m) tall. They are not quite as tall in temperate areas.

North America

Europe

Asia

Africa

South America

Australasia

Most animals in grasslands eat grass. In some places they sleep, or hibernate, when it gets cold in winter. You can read about some animals that live in grasslands in this book.

LION

Lions are predators. They live in tropical grasslands in Africa. A group of lions is called a pride. A male lion is the head of the pride.

A male lion has a **thick**, hairy mane.

Female lions do most of the hunting. They work together to catch an antelope or zebra. When they kill an animal, all the lions in the pride eat it.

ZEBRA

Zebras live in African grasslands.

They stay together in **big** herds.

The animals in the herd graze on grass.

WOW!

Every zebra has a different pattern of stripes.

Zebras don't sleep unless they are in a herd. The herd keeps watch for hunters such as lions. If a lion **attacks** a zebra, other zebras gather round to protect it.

ELEPHANT

African elephants are the **biggest** land animals. An elephant's trunk is a **l o n g** nose. The elephant uses it to smell, suck up water, and pick up food.

Elephants spray themselves with water to keep cool.

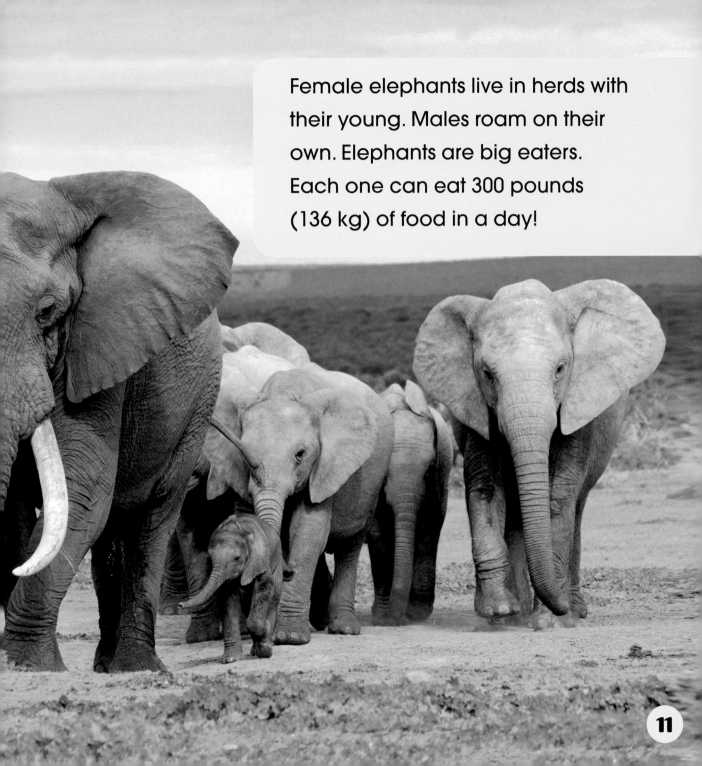

Female elephants live in herds with their young. Males roam on their own. Elephants are big eaters. Each one can eat 300 pounds (136 kg) of food in a day!

VULTURE

Vultures live all over the world. They feed on carrion—the bodies of dead animals.

In Africa, vultures wait for a lion to finish eating. Then they eat the rest of the kill.

A vulture does not have feathers on its head or neck.

This owl has white eyebrows and yellow eyes.

BURROWING OWL

These owls live in North and South America. They live in burrows underground. Sometimes they take over a hole made by another animal. The owls come out of their burrows to feed. They eat insects, mice, birds, and lizards.

CHEETAH

The cheetah lives in Africa. It has a spotted coat. This helps it hide in long grass when it is hunting. Cheetahs catch antelopes and hares. They have very sharp eyesight.

WOW!
Cheetahs drink every three or four days.

This **big** cat is the *fastest* land animal in the world. It can run at 60 mph (96 kph)!

WILDEBEEST

This animal has a **big** head with sharp, curving horns. It has a shaggy mane.

A wildebeest can be 4.5 feet (1.4 m) tall. It can weigh 600 pounds (272 kg).

A calf can walk minutes after it is born.

These animals live in **huge** herds. They spend most of their time grazing on grass. Between April and June every year, many wildebeest walk north to find food.

HYENA

Hyenas often eat dead animals. They are also skilled hunters. They work as a pack to hunt and *kill* a large animal. This might be a wildebeest or an antelope.

Hyenas also eat birds, lizards, snakes, and insects.

Hyenas can run fast for a long time.

These horses grow longer and thicker coats in winter.

PRZEWALSKI'S HORSE

These are the last wild horses left in the world. They live in Asia. These horses have short, **strong** bodies and a brown coat. They have a dark mane that stands upright and a white nose. They eat grasses and other green plants.

PRAIRIE DOG

Prairie dogs live in North America. They are not dogs at all! They are ground squirrels about the size of rabbits.

Most prairie dogs sleep, or hibernate, through the winter.

Prairie dogs say "hello" with a kiss or nuzzle.

Prairie dogs live in big burrows underground. Inside are lots of rooms and tunnels. Birds of prey, foxes, mountain lions, and coyotes eat prairie dogs.

GRASSLANDS FACTS

Grasslands grow in places where there is not enough rain for forests to grow.

Tropical grasslands grow in warm places where there is a lot of rain for half the year and hardly any rain for the other half.

Temperate grasslands grow in places that are hot in summer and cold in winter.

Grasslands have many names. In Africa they are savanna. In South America they are pampas. In Central Asia they are steppes.

USEFUL WORDS

carrion

The dead bodies of animals.
Vultures and hyenas feed on carrion.

hibernate

To go into a deep sleep in winter.

predator

An animal that hunts
other animals for food.
The lion is a predator. →

prey

An animal hunted and eaten
by another animal. Antelopes
are the prey of lions.

FIND OUT MORE

A Day in the Life: Grassland Animals series, Raintree, 2012

A Day and Night on the Prairie Caroline Arnold, Picture Window Books, 2015

African Savannah Claire Llewellyn, Kingfisher Readers, 2015

Grasslands (Exploring Ecosystems) Alexis Roumanis, Av2 by Weigl, 2015

INDEX

Africa, African 5, 6, 8, 12, 14
Asia 19

burrows 13, 21

calf 16
carrion 12

graze, grazing 8, 17

herds 8, 9, 11, 17
hibernate 5, 20
horns 16
hunting 7, 14

mane 6, 16, 19

North America 4, 13, 20

prairies 4
predators 6
pride (of lions) 6, 7

sleep 9
South America 13

trunk 10